Working Through Mommy Issues

Loving Yourself Even Though She Didn't Like You

Soneakqua J. White

Soneakqua J. White

Copyright © 2019 by Soneakqua J. White.

All rights reserved.

No part of this book may be reproduced or transmitted in any form or by any means, electronic or mechanical, including photocopying, recording, or by any information storage and retrieval system, without permission in writing from the copyright author, except for the use of brief quotations in a book review.

Published in the United States by
Pen2Pad Ink Publishing.

ISBN: 978-1-970135-22-0 paperback
978-1-970135-23-7 e-book

Requests to publish work from this book or to contact the author should be sent to:
sjw@atthetablecounseling.com

Soneakqua J. White retains the rights to all images

Interior design: Pen2Pad Ink Publishing

Soneakqua J. White

This book is designed to help you deal with a mother who makes it difficult for you to care *for* and/or care *about* her. If you have ever asked yourself, "Why does my mother treat me the way she does?" this book is for you. If you have found yourself wanting to scream out, "Help, my mom doesn't like me!" this book is for you. If you spent the majority of your life trying to make your mother proud of you or just tried to survive being raised by her and you still have not succeeded...this book is for you. You will learn how to love yourself even though she didn't like you. You will learn to stop compromising your mental, physical, emotional and spiritual health to get someone who does not acknowledge your effort to love you. Take your power out of her hands and live!

DISCLAIMER

This book has been written for educational purposes only. It provides information only up to the publishing date therefore this book should be used as a guidance tool and not an ultimate source. Its purpose is to provide information but does not contain all information on the subject. More research on your part may be needed. Every effort has been made to make this book as accurate as possible. The author and publisher shall have no liability or responsibility to any person or entity regarding any loss or damage incurred, or alleged to have incurred, directly or indirectly, by the information contained in this book.

Contents

Introduction   9

Section 1: You Cannot Change Someone Who Does Not Want To Change

Session 1: To change or not to change   13
Session 2: Let me count the ways   16
Session 3: Dare I ask?   19

Section 2: See Your Mother For Who She Really Is

Session 1: Do you see what I see?   23
Session 2: The "nice-nasty" list   28
Session 3: Growing up with "Mommy Dearest"   30

Section 3: Let Go of The Mother You Wish You Had

Session 1: Let it go   33
Session 2: It's not me...it's you   35
Session 3: Is adoption still an option?   38

Section 4: Decide What Kind of Relationship You Can Have With The Mother You Were Dealt

Session 1: Decisions...decisions   41
Session 2: Pick your poison   44
Session 3: It's not selfish...it's self-care   46

Section 5: Know, Understand, Set and Keep Your Boundaries

Session 1: Mom's need boundaries too!   50
Session 2: A line in the sand   52
Session 3: Consequences and Repercussions   60

Section 6: Do Your Emotional Work

Session 1: My first love   63
Session 2: The best thing you never had   67
Session 3: The first step to freedom   73

Section 7: Believer's Buy-In

Session 1: Your mother is a Believer too and she still doesn't like you   80
Session 2: Honoring her should not bring dishonor to you   82
Session 3: You're still on the hook   86

Message From The Author   89
Need More Help?   90
Other Books by Soneakqua J. White   91
Get Connected   92

Introduction

Hello! And welcome to your process on *Working Through Mommy Issues*. This is a problem that's near and dear to my heart because I grew up watching the impact that my grandmother had on her children, my mother included. It angered me to see her manipulate and reject them; even more so, after finding out how she abandoned them all as children. I used to think my grandmother was in a class all by herself. But, unfortunately, becoming a psychotherapist opened my eyes to the fact that there is actually a whole class of women exactly like my grandmother. I realized there are so many of you out there struggling with these women as mothers.

I understand that not everyone will go to counseling, so I decided to write a book and online course about this issue. My first novel called, *A Time to Heal* is the basis for them. You do not need to have the book in order to take the course; however, if you'd like to have it you can get it on Amazon or anywhere else books are sold. I wrote *A Time to Heal* as a part of my own healing from the situation. I decided to publish the book because I wanted others to know that I see and understand your pain and I want you to know there is help.

But, even beyond the fiction novel and the online course, I felt like there were more of you that I needed to reach. So, I decided to create this book.

We've gotten accustomed to hearing and talking about "daddy issues" but we're a little behind the curve ball in talking about "mommy issues". However, I do believe that just as many of you out there have mommy issues as daddy issues if not more.

If what I have said so far is hitting home for you then today is the day everything changes. Today is the day you're going to learn how to live a healthy life and love yourself, even with a mother who doesn't like you. I'll say this several times throughout the book because I want you to get it. This is not a book about how to understand why your mother is the way she is or why she does what she does. This is a book designed to free you from letting who she is continue to affect who you are.

There are 7 sections in this book. Section 1 is about understanding that you cannot change someone who does not want to change or doesn't know they need to change. In section 2, you will work toward seeing your mother for who she really is. Section 3 is almost like a myth buster. You will learn to let go of the idea of the mother you want or think you should have. Section 4 is getting you prepared to make a decision on what kind of relationship you want to have with her or whether you even want one with her at all. In section 5, you will learn how to set appropriate boundaries. Get ready to do some much needed emotional work in section 6. Now, section 7 is different from the others in that it is written specifically for those of you who are Believers of Christ. If you're not Christian, you can choose to skip section 7 if you

Working Through Mommy Issues

like and you will have completed the books sessions and activities. However, there is useful information in that section for anyone reading this book whether you're a Believer or not. So, everyone would benefit by completing all seven sections.

Before we get started, you will need a journal or paper and pen while reading this. There is at least one activity, take-away and attainable skill in each section. Also, there are some sections where you can write directly on the pages of this workbook if you would like to.

There are key points that will be repeated in certain sections and throughout the book. This was done on purpose. If you hear something repeated, it means it's really important, so take note. Understandably, this is a very sensitive and painful topic. If at any point throughout this book it gets too difficult, please stop and gather your thoughts and feelings. If you need to seek counseling before, during or after reading this book please do so. This is ultimately about you and your healing. Now grab your journals and let's get started!

YOU CANNOT CHANGE SOMEONE WHO DOES NOT WANT TO CHANGE

Section 1 Session 1
To Change or Not to Change

A parent is not supposed to have favorites, but your mother does and it's clearly not you. Please understand that it is nothing that you have done or not done to make her love you less. The way she feels about you is all on her. You don't need to do more or less or be more or less than who you are. You cannot change someone who does not want to change or doesn't know they need to change. Your mother may be perfectly happy with who she is and have no intentions on doing anything differently. As much as you may want or need her to be someone else for you, she will not do it unless and until she wants to. This book is all about the mommy issues you have, but it applies to fathers too!

The only person you can change in this situation is yourself. You will not necessarily be able to turn off the desire you have for your mother to love you. But, if you have spent your life trying to get her attention or waited for her to change her heart toward you...stop! You are hurting yourself for someone who does not see your effort. There is nothing you can do because the problem did not begin with you. I know this may be hard to hear but unfortunately, this is not something you can fix.

You cannot work harder for the change than your mother does. I understand that you may want it more than she does, but you cannot make her change. You can only call her attention to it. She has to admit that she needs to change and then commit to doing the work to make the changes. In the meantime, you have to work on backing off from doing things that wear you out, only to be disappointed by her repeatedly. You are trying to be good, better and best for someone who has yet to see your worth. This is like drinking poison and hoping the other person will die. It's not going to turn out the way you want, so stop!

Since this is easier said than done, I have an assignment for you.

Activity:

Have your journal or paper and pen ready if you don't have enough lines below. Write down all the things you have done since you've been an adult to try to get your mother to notice you. For example, if you have taken her out to dinner, shopping, given her money or whatever you've done to try to get her to treat you better...write all of that down. Once you've listed everything you can remember, turn it all back on yourself. Pick one thing from the list that you will do for yourself today in order to please you and no one else. This is your first lesson in self-care. If the people you're consistently giving everything to do not appreciate it, then it is ok to give it to yourself.

Working Through Mommy Issues

Section 1 Session 2
Let Me Count the Ways

The way your mother feels about you is not something you can fix for several reasons. First of all, you don't know what's wrong. You may have an idea or other people may have even put their two cents in, but the truth is...unless she tells you herself, you really don't know. There are so many reasons why mother's treat their children indifferently or abuse them blatantly. Your mother could have had an issue with your father or his family that you never knew about. It's unfortunate, because it is something that happened before you were born that you are now paying the price for. It didn't have anything to do with you and that is why you can't fix it.

Perhaps your mother sees a lot of herself in you. She doesn't like herself and therefore she doesn't like you either. Again, it's not your fault. You can't help her fix the things she doesn't like about herself. That's up to her. It's absolutely unfair for you to have to deal with her issues, but it is the situation you're in. Generational dysfunction continues because of situations just like this; however, you're reading this book so that it doesn't continue in your life or the lives of your descendants.

It's possible that your mom didn't want kids, yet she gave birth to more than one. This is not the case for everyone, but for some moms, a child is equal to a paycheck. The way the welfare system is set up, you get rewarded for having kids that you can't take care of. And, if you make them "crazy" or give them a disability of some sort, you can get an extra check! They have some amazing services that regular working folk don't have access to; they get housing, food stamps, free college tuition...being a mom has benefits. It doesn't mean you actually have to love and parent the kids, you only have to have them. I'll say again, this is not the case for all. There are some moms that would not have been able to survive were it not for the welfare system. But, unfortunately there are some who abused the system and abused their children in the process.

Making a distinction between children is another huge issue that I see. As I mentioned in the first section, parents are not supposed to have favorites, but your mom does and it's clearly not you! You may never understand why the other children are treated better or differently than you. Does she like their father more? Do you remind her of your father whom she does not like? Is your personality too different? Are you too unique for her taste? You could ask yourself a million questions and I'm sure you have. But, you have to stop asking. Because the truth is that she may never tell you and if you knew the answer you might wish you never asked.

Take Away:

If you remember nothing else, remember that your mother not liking you has nothing to do with you. She is battling her own demons and it is being taken out on you. That may not make you feel any better, but it does let you off the hook as far as trying to fix the problem. It's not yours to fix. You cannot carry guilt, shame or blame for something you had nothing to do with.

Section 1 Session 3
Dare I Ask?

Many of you have only questioned yourselves about why your mother treats you the way she does. But I know there are some of you that have asked her directly. If you have already confronted her, ask yourself how it went. Did she admit that she treats you differently than your other siblings? Did she admit that she does not care for you? Was she honest?

Did she blow you off or curse you out? If so, please understand she is angry because she likely didn't realize that you were aware or on to her. She disliked being confronted because admitting to not liking one of her children reveals that she is not a good person. She likely wants to be seen by others as someone she's really not. She does not want to talk about it because she would have to admit to how poorly she has treated a person she gave birth to. Her anger may also be because she couldn't believe that you would have the audacity to confront her. She may have always seen you as weak, but clearly, she was wrong.

Be careful or the blame will be on you. You may be considered ungrateful for opening your mouth to say such a thing about your own mother. You may have been told that you were crazy for even thinking or saying something like that. After all, she kept you and raised you didn't she?

Did she act like a victim? Was she dramatic, like she was being accused of something so horrific that she had to clutch her pearls in disbelief? She may have even conjured up some tears. You may have to endure being reminded of all the things she's ever done for you and your children, if you have them. How could you think she didn't love you after everything she sacrificed? She may get other people involved at this point to be on her side. You may become the villain simply by asking the question, so be prepared.

If you have not yet said anything to your mother, do not confront her until you have finished this book. It will ensure that you are better prepared for the confrontation. As you can see from everything mentioned, you could get thrown off by an avalanche of emotions on both sides. So do not do this until you are ready.

Attainable Skill:

In preparation for the day of confrontation, I want you to consider using "I" statements. This is also a good idea for those of you who desire to try to have that conversation again as well. Be specific in what you say and only bring up concrete scenarios. For example, if you said, "You hurt my feelings when you invited everyone over except for me!" In her mind, you're already in your feelings. So, guess what she's going to do? Right, she's going to dismiss your feelings. Instead, try saying, "I feel hurt when my other siblings are invited over for dinner and I don't get invited. Like last Sunday, I looked for everyone and they were all at your house...everyone except me." Beginning a sentence with "I" instead of "you" helps keep the defensiveness down.

Section 2 Session 1
Do You See What I See?

You know the relationship between your mother and you better than anyone else. Be honest with yourself about who she is to you and how she is toward you. Your thoughts and feelings are valid and real. Whoever she is to you is your truth, no matter how she shows herself to others.

Do not try to get others on your side because they may never see it your way. Typically, we do this to try to validate our own thoughts and feelings. We want others to see it how we see it, so we know for sure that it is what it is. What I'm telling you is that you have the right to think how you think and feel how you feel. If others are telling you that it's in your head, then you owe it to yourself to do your best to find out if that's the case or not. However, this is not something you should ask someone who knows you or your mother because they may be biased. This is the time when you want to seek outside and possibly professional help. It needs to be someone who is looking at the situation from a completely different unbiased vantage point.

It is quite possible and very likely that your mother is two different people. She may be one way with you and completely the opposite toward others and/or especially when others are around. One way behind closed doors and another way in public. This behavior is not uncommon for manipulative and abusive individuals. You may have a mother that makes sure others don't see how she behaves towards you. Then on the flip side, you may have a mother who shows a blatant dislike for you and everybody knows it. But, whatever type of mother you have, it is important that you believe her actions toward you and not what she says. I always say, "When people show you who they are, believe them."

Activity:

For this activity, complete the questionnaire on the following page. There are no right or wrong answers. There is not a certain number that you need to answer "yes" or "no" to. However, if you answer "yes" to more than five questions, there are some major concerns with the relationship between you and your mother. If you have not talked to anyone about the answers to your questions yet, you would benefit from doing so. Again, I'm making the suggestion that you talk to someone outside the family. Please take the time to complete this activity as you will need to refer to it in an upcoming section.

Section 2 Session 1 Activity:

Are my thoughts and feelings valid?

☐ Yes ☐ No Has your mother ever talked down to you in public or in private?

☐ Yes ☐ No Have you ever felt rejected by your mother?

☐ Yes ☐ No Has your mother ever threatened to or actually physically assaulted you?

☐ Yes ☐ No Does she act one way with your siblings and another way with you?

☐ Yes ☐ No Do you now or have you ever had a fear of your mother?

☐ Yes ☐ No Does your mother curse you out?

☐ Yes ☐ No Do you avoid communicating with your mother or wish you could?

☐ Yes ☐ No Has she ever put you out of her home or made you want to leave?

☐ Yes ☐ No Has she ever excluded you from activities your siblings were invited to?

☐ Yes ☐ No Have you ever made excuses for the way your mother treats you?

☐ Yes ☐ No Do you feel obligated to do things for her even when you don't want to?

☐ Yes ☐ No Can your siblings get away with things concerning her that you can't?

☐ Yes ☐ No Would you say that you and your mother have a love/hate relationship?

☐ Yes ☐ No Have you spent the majority of your life trying to get her to like/love you?

☐ Yes ☐ No Are you having trouble accepting the person your mother is to you?

☐ Yes ☐ No Are you typically the one who has to be the "bigger person"?

☐ Yes ☐ No Do you believe your mother needs to change?

☐ Yes ☐ No Do you need to heal from the mental/emotional damage she has caused?

☐ Yes ☐ No Do you wonder what life would

have been like with another mother?

☐ Yes ☐ No Have you ever asked yourself what you did so wrong?

Section 2 Session 2
The 'Nice-Nasty' List

Let's dig a little deeper into finding out who your mother really is. Have you ever heard the term "nice-nasty"? Well, if you have the type of mom who manipulates to get what she wants, then this is the term you might use. She's nice and pleasant on the surface, but has under-handed or ill intentions. It may look to other people that she keeps in constant contact with you because she loves you so much. She sends text, she calls, she invites you over, etc. But, if anyone knew what she actually said to you during those textversations, phone conferences or home visits, they would hurt for you. She is nice on the surface and nasty underneath.

It's manipulative to lure your children into doing or not doing something under false pretenses. Similarly, it's also manipulative to guilt or shame your children into doing or not doing something. Gut check, if you are feeling guilty, shamed or obligated to do something for your mother then you are likely being manipulated. This is something that is being done to you because she believes she can get away with it. She has been doing this for so long that you don't even realize it, but you're getting tired of feeling this way. It's time for you to pick up on it when it's happening and change the way you respond to it.

If your mother has been manipulating you all your life it's because you're a good target. This is likely because you have always had something to lose by not allowing yourself to be manipulated. Often, children of manipulative and/or abusive parents struggle with people pleasing. You want their love so badly you would do just about anything to get it. You are constantly trying to work to get love, attention and affection. The problem is that you shouldn't have to work for it. A mother who really loves her children would never make her love for them conditional.

Take-Away:

If your mother's love for you has conditions to it, she makes the "nice-nasty" list. There are some very strong boundaries that will need to be put up in order to allow yourself to better cope. You may need to cut back on some of the phone calls, home visits or whatever way you communicate with her. Yes, it is ok to cut the time you spend on your mom back! Listen, I know what you're thinking. I know it's your mother and you love her. But, this is also part of the problem. You love her so much that you are willing to hurt yourself to keep in contact with her. You have to stop.

Section 2 Session 3
Growing up with 'Mommy Dearest'

Mommy Dearest was almost like a female Dr. Jekyll and Mr. Hyde. We'll call her Dr. Jackie and Mrs. Hyde. She wanted children, but she wanted perfect children to go along with her "perfect" lifestyle. As long as everything was going like she wanted it to go, she was Dr. Jackie. Glamourous and beautiful with a wonderful daughter who was her pride and joy. But as soon as just one thing was out of order, she turned into something more like Mrs. Hyde. She would wake the child up in the middle of the night to clean an entire bathroom merely because she found one speck of dirt!

If your mother was or is like this, you may struggle with anxiety simply because you never knew or still never know who you're going to get. If she was or is emotionally, physically or verbally abusive, then you may have darker thoughts and feelings towards her. It may now seem normal to you, but I submit to you that being abused by your mother or anyone else for that matter is not normal! You have the right to protect yourself. If you are reading this book and you are still being abused, please seek professional help immediately. If you have insurance, you can call your insurance company to get a list of names for counseling. If you do not have insurance, you can simply Google what you want or go to verified websites like Psychology Today. Whatever method you choose to find the information, get it now!

Even if the abuse took place in the past, you likely still need to seek professional help. You may not realize that how you were treated by your mother has shaped the way you function in relationships now. But, you will have to admit that you had and may still have a manipulative or abusive mother. You cannot and will not recover from her mistreatment unless and until you can admit to who she really is. You cannot conquer what you do not confront!

Attainable Skill:

You really need to know how to find a counselor for yourself should you decide you need one. Contact your insurance company to get a list of names of counselors that you could see. Also, contact your HR department to find out if you have an Employee Assistance Program (EAP). This will give you counseling sessions at no expense to you. It also includes any family member that lives in your household.

LET GO OF THE MOTHER YOU WISH YOU HAD

Section 3 Session 1
Let It Go

You probably have your ideal mother in your head, but the one you actually have is the complete opposite. One of the most difficult things I'm going to ask you to do is to let go of that "ideal" mother. She might actually exist, but she's not the one you have. You have to deal with reality. You cannot wish your mother away or wish her into being someone else. She is who she is choosing to be. You will have to accept who she is and figure out how you want to manage your responses to who she is.

In the previous section, you had to see your mother for who she is. Now, you have to accept her for who she is. You've acknowledged who she is. Now you have to accept her. By acceptance, I do not mean you have to put up with everything she says or does. I just mean that since you now see her for who actually she is, whether she's "nice-nasty", Mommy Dearest or Mrs. Hyde, whoever she is...accept that you see the truth of who you're dealing with. You're going to need to learn how to handle whoever it is that you're working with. Acceptance is basically saying, "this is the hand I've been dealt." You don't get to throw that hand back in; you have to learn to play that hand.

The better you know, understand and accept her, the better you will get in knowing how you want to handle her. Remember that this book is really all about you. Your mother might need help, but she either doesn't know it or doesn't want it. Either way, that's not your problem. You are working on how to manage the mother you have and the only variable you can change is you. You are going to have to look at her through different eyes. Not from the eyes of a child who still wants and needs a mommy, but from the perspective of an adult learning to work with another adult.

Take Away:

Accepting who you have as a mother is not the same thing as putting up with it. Accepting her means understanding that you will not change her and that you will have to develop a game plan as to how you're going to handle who and what you have.

Section 3 Session 2
It's Not Me...It's You

It's not your fault that your mother is the way she is. No matter what she says, it's not about you. There is nothing you can do or stop doing to make her treat you differently. You may have been trying to figure it out all your life with no luck, even if she's told you what you've "done". It doesn't make sense to you and it's not something you can change.

Chances are that your mother developed a dislike for you because of something that happened before you were born or conceived. Maybe she wasn't ready to have a baby and she was forced to have you. Maybe she can't stand your father. It could be any number of things, but the only one that matters to you is that you didn't cause it. That's why you can't fix it. It's not your problem. Yes, it absolutely does affect you and it's completely unfair. But the truth is that it's not even about you. You just got caught in the crossfire. The great thing is that you can remove yourself. You can change your position.

You are in control of how you respond to her. If you are still allowing her to control your responses, then you may have to back away until you are able to get yourself under control. Chances are that she has gotten accustomed to the way you react to things and it's not difficult for her to push your buttons. Regardless of whether she is purposefully trying to or not, she is really good at getting you to react out of emotion. I'm not blaming you for it. There should be no shame because of it. What I'm telling you is that you have to stop allowing her to control you and your emotions. It's hurting you.

For most abusers and manipulators, it's all about control. If they cannot control you then there is no reward there for them. So, once you start taking back your control, you will likely see one of three behaviors. One, she will become a bit more aggressive or ugly towards you because she can't get you to do what she wants when she wants any more. You're going to make her angry. Two, you may see her become a bit more manipulative in playing a victim type of role in order to guilt you. Or three, she will completely back away from you, reject and abandon you because you are no longer of any use to her. Whatever happens, you need to be prepared.

Attainable Skills:

Get out your journal and write this down or write on the lines below. Think about some of the occasions where your mother was able to negatively effect your emotions. A time you cried, got angry, depressed or withdrawn. Think about how you could have handled the situation differently for yourself. Using those situations, come up with 3 statements or behaviors you will use in order to protect or release yourself from any situation your mother attempts to trap you in. See it before it happens and respond in a way that keeps you out of harms' way. She doesn't likely have any new tricks. So, anything that she's done in the past she will probably try again. Should it happen again, you'll be ready for her.

_____

_____

_____

_____

_____

_____

_____

_____

_____

_____

_____

_____

_____

Section 3 Session 3
Is Adoption Still an Option?

I bet I know what you're thinking at this point. If I stop allowing her to control me then I won't have a relationship with her at all. Then I won't have a mother. Have you considered a surrogate? I can almost guarantee there is another woman in your life who would be an amazing stand-in for your mother; someone who wants to love you and be good to you. It could be an aunt, an older cousin or it might even be someone who's not related to you at all. If you could allow yourself the opportunity of having a surrogate mother, then you would not have to long for a mother you can't and unfortunately don't have.

Now that you're an adult you have more choices. DNA may make you related, but relationship makes you family. Your mother will always be your mother and nothing can change that. However, you now have the option to decide what part she plays in your life. You can decide to allow another mother figure into your life. You're not stuck. Sure, your mother might be jealous, but it will be ok even if she is. This is not about her. It's about you and what you need. She hasn't been able to or hasn't wanted to give you what you need. She will have to stand by and know that someone else is doing it for you. Do not allow your mother to treat you worse because of your surrogate.

At this point, you don't owe her anything. You owe it to yourself to be happy.

No one will ever be able to take the place of your biological mother. You might always have the hope and desire for her to change and become the mother you always wanted. But, you cannot wait around for something that may or may not ever happen. It's ok for you to enjoy your life now. Having a surrogate mom to talk to, go shopping with, vacation, go to lunch with and do all the things you can't do with your mother may lessen the sting. It will allow you to live your life without as many regrets. Of course, there will always be a special spot in your heart for your mother. However, a surrogate could make it so that you don't have to go without a mother figure in your life if you don't want to.

Activity:

Here's another activity I have for you to do. Get a sheet a paper or you can use your journal. Draw a line down the center. On the left side, write down all the characteristics you wish your mom had. On the right side, write down the characteristics that your mom actually has. Think about the people in your life who possess the characteristics on the left. These are the people you utilize as surrogates. You can have more than one. There's no need to put pressure on just one person to be all things. Allow yourself the freedom of others being there for you. There's no need for you to be alone if you don't want to.

Section 4 Session 1
Decisions...Decisions

The first question you need to ask yourself is, "Do I want to have a relationship with my mother?" If the answer is "no" then you can skip the rest of this section and the next and jump to Section 6. However, if you do want a relationship with your mother, then here is where you have some tough decisions to make. You have to evaluate the current relationship to understand what kind of relationship is feasible for you. At this time, we can only go on the assumption that your mother will make no changes in her behavior. If this remains the case, you have to ask yourself, "What kind of healthy relationship could I possibly have with her?" Healthy has to be a part of the equation. Because if you are reading this book, then it is highly likely that your current relationship is unhealthy, at least from your viewpoint.

When dealing with others, sometimes there's not a sure-fire way to never have any pain in the relationship. Feelings can get hurt, but if there is effective communication, things can be mended. Hopefully you completed the checklist in Section 2. If you haven't, please pause here and do so now. It begins on page 25. If you have already completed it, please look over the list of questions and remind yourself of the things you answered "yes" to. In a healthy relationship you should honestly be able to answer "no" to the "yes" questions. Seeing that you have no control over your mother, ask yourself how you will handle these situations in a healthy manner. Is it even possible? Should you even have a relationship with her if all of this is still going on? Is there any way you can work through or avoid these particular situations? Ask yourself if continuing a relationship with your mother will be more harmful than good.

Be honest with yourself about what you are willing to deal with. It's not a matter of what you can tolerate, because you've been attempting to hang in there for a long time. What I'm asking you to determine is should you? You are attempting to heal and get healthy for yourself. Continuing to put yourself in a toxic environment will only hinder your progress and may even make things worse. When you are making the decisions of whether or not to move forward in a relationship, you must consider your consequences.

Activity:

Grab some paper, your journal, or write on the lines below. Think about what you would consider 5 characteristics of a healthy relationship between a mother and an adult child? Write those down. If you are having difficulty coming up with healthy characteristics, look back at your checklist to help you. You can use the opposite of the questions or statements on the checklist. I'll also remind you of the hint I gave you from a previous section. If the communication is effective between you, it will go a long way in solving any issues that may arise. Keep in mind even while writing down your healthy characteristics, no relationship is perfect, but it should at least be healthy.

___

___

___

___

___

___

___

___

___

___

___

Section 4 Session 2
Pick Your Poison

Can you have a relationship with your mother without causing yourself more damage? If your mother creates a toxic environment for you, then you really need to consider how much poison you can handle. If you've decided that you want to try and have a relationship with her, what type of relationship can you have? What will she allow? What will you allow yourself to put up with?

Please understand that you are at risk when playing with fire like this. Keeping yourself in a toxic environment for the sake of trying to have a relationship with someone is like you drinking poison and hoping the other person will die. The ultimate consequence of poison is death. It may not be a physical death, but a spiritual or emotional death can cause a lifetime of damage.

Think about the types of situations you've been in with her where everything appears to be ok. Are there any occasions where she is nice to you or at least cordial? Focus on those events and avoid the ones where you are typically mistreated. If she treats you better when a certain person is around, then try to ensure that person is available when it's time to be in the presence of your mother. Does she put on her best fake self at church? Then you know it's safe to go to church with her, but maybe not lunch afterwards.

Whenever you are going to be at an event with your mother, you always need a plan of escape. If you can avoid it, do not put yourself in a position where you will be stuck with her. Drive your own car to events so that you can leave whenever you need to. Know what you will say or do when it's time for you to leave and do not let anyone talk you into staying longer than you feel comfortable. Always try to leave the situation on a happy note, if at all possible.

Take Away:

Let me reiterate this point. Know your safe events and escapes. Plan ahead. Do not allow yourself to be talked into or out of anything you have already planned for your safety and security. It may be difficult to leave when things are going well, but you always want to leave on a good note. Therefore, do not overstay your visits.

Section 4 Session 3
It's Not Selfish...It's Self-Care

It may be very difficult for you to change your behaviors when it comes to your mother. This is the part where your head may have to fight your heart and prevail. It can be confusing to think about distancing yourself from your own mother, even when you know you might need to. After all, she's still your mother and the only one you have. However, this is a person in your life who has caused you pain for most of it. You are not trying to punish her by making the decisions you're making. You're trying to release yourself. You may be called selfish when you start implementing some of the things you're going to have to implement. And in all of it, whatever you decide, I want you to remember that it's not selfish...it's self-care.

You are going to have to put your thoughts and feelings ahead of hers during this time because you need to figure out what's right for you. No one can dictate to you about your needs. You have to give yourself a fair chance to figure out what your needs are. There will be some who will not understand the change in your behavior toward your mother. Remember, they may not experience her behavior the way you do. She may not treat everyone else like she treats you. These are going to be some tough decisions that you are going to have to make without a whole lot of input from others, unless they can see it from your perspective.

Not everyone will commend you for the decisions you are about to make. But, you're not looking for commendation. You are looking for peace. If your relationship with your mother disturbs your peace, then you have to change it. If she is not willing to change her behavior, then you have no choice but to change yours. That is, if you want to be better after you finish this book than you were before it. We will talk more about this in Section 6, but as I mentioned in a previous section, going to counseling is not a bad idea. It will give you a fresh pair of ears and a non-biased sounding board. If you don't want to go to counseling, then find a non-judgmental friend or use your journal. But, work this out.

Attainable Skill:

Know that there will be those who will call you selfish. I want to talk to you about the differences between selfish and self-care. Selfish is one who typically looks out for themselves and their own interests regardless of what others might think or feel about the situation. As long as it benefits them they will do it. Whereas self-care is giving yourself some of the same attention you give to others. If others deserve to be pampered or catered to, then so do you. You cannot live your life only giving and never replenishing. If you are unable to receive it from others, you will have to give it to yourself. And yes, it is ok to give to yourself. That's not selfish, that's self-care.

KNOW, UNDERSTAND, SET AND KEEP YOUR BOUNDARIES

Section 5 Session 1
Mom's Need Boundaries Too!

If you are going to continue in a relationship with your mother, then there needs to be some boundaries set. Yes, moms need boundaries too! You are the one who gets to decide what they are and you are the one who has to enforce them. It's not a question of whether or not you need to set boundaries with your mom; it's a matter of what kind.

Your boundary is your cutoff point. It lets others know what you will and will not tolerate. Setting boundaries is necessary in every area of life. If you don't have any, it can give the illusion that you will put up with anything. I have a feeling that some of you think you should put up with anything, especially when it's coming from your mother. But, let me tell you that it's not true.

When you appropriately set a boundary, you are showing people how to respect you, your thoughts and your feelings. You also allow them to make a decision as to whether or not they want to be in your life. As you will see in Session 3 of this section, there are consequences to be upheld if the boundaries are crossed. Allowing people to make their own decisions will take the pressure off you.

Your desire is that setting the boundaries with your mother will be of some benefit to you both. The hope is that your boundaries would force her to modify her behavior. But, you are more so doing it for your own sake. Even if nothing changes with her, you are no longer allowing yourself to be hurt by things that she says or does. You are going to modify your behavior no matter what. You will have to work through the desire to not make the changes and you will have to work through the emotions of having to do the things you're going to have to do. Understanding that boundaries are needed is one thing. Setting them and enforcing them is a whole other matter.

Take Away:

Everyone in your life needs to have boundaries, including your mother. She does not get a free pass just because she gave birth to you. This is not a matter of being disrespectful. Setting boundaries will become a part of helping you to honor her. It may not feel like it at the onset, but there will be a difference made. Yes, there will be some struggle with doing this if it's not something you're accustomed to. But, trust me, it's necessary. Setting boundaries will teach you how to command the respect you deserve.

Section 5 Session 2
A Line in the Sand

What type of boundaries may need to be set? This will be different for each person reading this book, because it will depend on the particular issues you have with your mother. Think about whether or not there are issues with communication, behavior, money, etc. These are the indicators you will use in order to set your boundaries. You may have several boundaries that you will have to set according to what you want to correct.

It's possible you may need boundaries surrounding communication. For example, if you don't like when she curses at you, set the boundary. Let her know that if she curses at you that you will discontinue the conversation; whether that means no longer responding to a text, hanging up the phone or physically removing yourself from her presence. This is what you will do if she curses at you. Use this same reference for any other boundaries you need to set with her as well.

For those of you who have money issues with your mother, this is going to be really important but really touchy. If you cannot afford to pay your bills and hers too, please do not allow anyone to make you feel bad about that. Set the boundary. Give her an allowance and inform her that there will be no extra support. Let her know that you will only be able to give her a set amount of money each month and she will have to learn how to budget. If she has a problem with not spending the money on what she's supposed to spend it on, then you can choose pay the bill for her instead of handing out money. The key is that you will not be a revolving door or an ATM.

Keep in mind that this situation may be harder on you than it will be on her, especially if she is manipulative. She probably knows how to make you feel bad about not giving her money. She may do something like spending her money on whatever she wants and expect you to buy her groceries because she spent her grocery money. Or, she may do whatever she wants and then call you in a "panic" because the electricity bill didn't get paid and her lights are going to be cut off if you don't pay it. This is where it gets tough for you because no one wants their mother to go hungry or without electricity. It will be hard, but trust me. She didn't just become manipulative when you were born. If you don't do it, I promise she will figure out how to get it done. You will just have to be willing to let her do it without your help.

Once you have set the boundaries within yourself, then you have to actually state the boundaries to your mother. This is not something that you will have to do all at one time. You do not need to have a five-hour conversation to set one hundred boundaries. Take the time to think about the ones you know you need to set up front. Then, as others arise you have the conversation then and there or whenever it is convenient. It is highly important that you warn your mother about the things she's doing before you enforce a consequence. You do not want her to become the victim and try to make you feel guilty for a consequence that she didn't know about.

Activity:

For your next activity, you will have a chance to practice working through at least one boundary you need to set. Then think about the best times to start talking to your mother to get them set. Hold off on having the conversations until you have finished the book and possibly met with a counselor. You want to make sure you are ready to do this. Because the worse thing you can do aside from not setting a boundary at all, is setting one and not enforcing it. Your activity begins on page 56. You can write directly in your book or use your journal. Follow the example given to you and then create your own.

_____

_____

_____

_____

_____

Working Through Mommy Issues

Section 5 Session 2 Activity
Boundary Setting

Boundary Topic: Ex: Communication

_____

_____

_____

_____

_____

_____

_____

_____

_____

_____

Working Through Mommy Issues

Issue: Ex: My mom curses at me and I don't like it.

New Boundary: Ex: I will not tolerate anyone cursing at me including my mother.

Consequence: Ex: If she curses at me, I will discontinue communication, whether it is by not responding to text, disconnecting the phone call or physically removing myself from her presence.

_____

_____

_____

_____

_____

_____

_____

_____

_____

_____

_____

_____

_____

_____

Section 5 Session 3
Consequences and Repercussions

Probably the most important thing you have to do when setting boundaries is to follow through. Most people set boundaries and never follow through. If you do that, it will be as if you never set the boundary for some. For others it will be worse because you tried it with no bite behind it and now you look weak. Your mother already has a certain level of disrespect and dislike for you, because if she didn't, she wouldn't treat you the way she does. Do not give her any more reason to think less of you. Do not initiate your boundaries with her until you're ready to enforce them.

There must be a consequence if the boundaries are crossed. If you don't, you will lose more respect than you ever had if you ever had any at all. You do not want to get into a situation where you allow people to see that you have no follow through. If your mother will respect you enough to operate within your boundaries, your relationship will get better because she will learn not to do the things you're asking her not to. However, if she repeatedly crosses your boundaries, she will make the decision for you to cut her off without you having to do it. You teach people how to treat you. If they don't want to learn, don't make that your problem. Why worry yourself over someone who has no respect for you. There would be no need for you to feel guilty about something she did to herself. Either way, you're changing the way you respond to her and you're changing the way you allow yourself to be treated.

Standing up for yourself is not something your mother will likely respond well to coming from you. However, you may find that she might respect you for it. You just don't know until you do it. But, remember that this is about you. You will respect yourself more if you stop allowing yourself to be run over and hurt, just because it's coming from your mother. Your thoughts and feelings are not any less or any more important than hers, except when it comes to you. You need to do what's best for you. And what's best for you no longer includes being torn down by her.

Attainable Skill:

Stand your ground. Stick to the boundaries you have set once you have set them. Rehearse the conversation you will have with your mother, keeping in mind that it doesn't matter how she feels about it. They are your boundaries and it is how YOU want it. But, you will likely be tested especially if she doesn't agree. You might even be tested because she may not believe you have the strength or the courage to enforce it. You must enforce the consequences or nothing will change. Be on the lookout for the test, because it will happen. You need to pass the test.

DO YOUR EMOTIONAL WORK

Section 6 Session 1
My First Love

Whether you have decided to have any kind of relationship with your mother or not, there is a great deal of emotional work that needs to be done on your part. You must heal from the damage that was caused over the years. You may have been able to deal with it and continue to progress in life. You have aged chronologically, but there are likely some places you did not grow in emotionally. If you are honest with yourself, there are some things in your life that you are not pleased with. Not that every issue you've had in life was caused by your mother, but there are likely paths that you would have chosen to do differently had it not been for the type of relationship or lack of a relationship you had with her.

A mother is the first person who shows us how to be loved. She is the first one to show us affection and genuine interest. She is the one who meets our needs even when we cannot convey them. However, if you did not receive the love, care, attention and affection you needed, you likely grew up with built-in self-esteem issues that you are still battling with today. You are possibly an overachiever, a people pleaser, a selfless caretaker and/or a person who has a difficult time saying "no" to helping others. Many of you might be what one of my good friends Amber would call a pineapple; hard and prickly on the outside and soft and sweet on the inside. You have a tough exterior because you had to grow up faster than you should have. You had to protect your thoughts, feelings and emotions because when you didn't you got hurt or disappointed. You appear to never need help. You may be one of those people that everybody goes to because you know a lot and seem to be able to handle anything. But, you are really a sweetheart on the inside. Even when you could use some help and probably need it you don't ask for it; however, you are always willing to give it. You cannot stand to see anyone suffer. Your heart hurts for other people, because you were hurt so badly inside that you would never want anyone else to feel the way you do. Except when it comes to you...you hide that part.

It's not a bad thing to be a selfless person. The problem with it is that you suffer greatly and you do it in silence. You are worn out, but you continue to try to keep going. Your mind, body and spirit are all begging for you to rest and yet you still keep going. Here's where the problem with your mother rears its ugly head. If you did not get the love from her you needed, you are likely not a good lover of yourself. You try to give everyone else what you did not get from her. You try to ensure that no one ever feels what you had to feel. You don't want anyone to struggle with the emptiness, the loneliness, or the rejection you felt. You would never want anyone to think they were unwanted or unloved because that's the way she made you feel. Here's where your emotional work begins. Your mother was supposed to be your first love, but she wasn't. Now, you must figure out how to love yourself and know that you are worthy of the love she didn't give.

Activity:

Here's what I want you to do. Of course, you'll need your journal or paper. Write down this journaling prompt:

(1) What do you think about yourself? Now, most of the time when we think about this question, we tend to say what other people would say about us. What I'm asking you to do is clear out all the other thoughts and voices that are not your own and I want you to tell me what YOU think of YOURSELF. It's not meant to be easy and it may not be positive, but I want you to tell the truth. After you finish writing out those thoughts, I want you to move to the next prompt.

_____

_____

_____

_____

_____

_____

(2) If 200 years from now high school students were reading about you in the history books, what would you want to be remembered for? Take your time in doing these activities. The next session will wait for you.

_____

_____

_____

_____

_____

_____

_____

_____

_____

_____

_____

_____

Section 6 Session 2
The Best Thing You Never Had

In order to heal and really begin to love yourself, you may have to go through a grieving process. You are going to grieve the mother you always wanted but never had. This process really does not have a time limit and does not necessarily follow a sequential order. You may even experience some things outside of the process I'm about to explain. Just know that you have a right to your own thoughts and feelings. And even though most of them will be very unpleasant, it is all a part of the process. I have already mentioned this on a couple of other occasions in other sections, but you may need to go through some counseling to assist in this process because it can become quite overwhelming and at times very painful.

When grieving, there is often a period of denial and/or isolation. This will look different for different people, but this is where you're faced with the hand you were dealt as it comes to mothers. You cannot believe you got stuck with the one you have! You see others with these great moms and you don't understand why you couldn't have one like them. This is also where you might start to blame yourself. You might think "my mom could not be this bad...She's not this bad to other people. Maybe it's me. Maybe if

I were different then she would be better...and so and so on." But, remember we've already talked about this. Your mother's behavior is not your fault. There is nothing that you can start or stop doing that would make her change the way she feels about you. This is your own denial talking because you just don't want to see YOUR mother as the person she truly is.

You might be tempted to think that if you could get your mom to hang around some of your friends' moms, then it's possible it would influence her to be different. Your hope is that maybe they'll rub off on her. Honestly, you've been bargaining with her your whole life. You may not say anything out loud, but you're making deals with your behavior. You're thinking, well if I do this, then she'll do that and everything will be great! If I stop doing this, then she won't do that and everything will be great! Did you know that bargaining is actually a part of the grieving process? You wouldn't have to do this if your mother treated you the way you needed her to. This is just another way of trying not to accept the fact that she is who she is. If you have to bribe her to be who you want her to be, then it's not genuine.

You get angry with her as well. You might struggle with this, because who wants to be angry with their mother? But, the truth is that you are. She has hurt you for a very long time and you're not even asking for much. You just want her to like you; to treat you like a human being that she cares for. You keep trying to trust her with your heart and she keeps disappointing you, she keeps hurting you. Anger is a normal human emotion. It's ok to be angry with your mother, but it's not ok to stay there. You have to get down to the real emotion and deal with it. It's hurt.

Depression is always looming in a situation like this. Anxiety is not too far from the depression either. When your foundation starts off shaky, it usually continues to be unstable unless there is an intervention. If you grew up with a mother who didn't like you, then your foundation was shaky. You likely made some decisions in your life that you regret, because you were either trying to please her or get away from her.

Unresolved past issues can often lead to depression. Anxiety is more about the fear of the future. Never having a steady foundation is a good recipe for anxiety, because you never know if you're ok. You're never quite sure that you're good enough if no other parental figure picks up the slack and tells you that you are. Sure, you can make things happen. You are in charge. No one has to know that you have no confidence in yourself. All they know is that you can get it done. They rarely see that you're dying inside, because they're so used to you going on like nothing is wrong, even when your life is completely falling apart on the inside.

You won't allow yourself to sit down long enough to admit that you're depressed. You just refuse to think until the thoughts intrude on their own. Intrusive thoughts are often indicators that you're in trouble. What do I mean by intrusive thoughts? You know the ones that say things like... "If you ran your car off this bridge nobody would even miss you...If your own mother doesn't love you then who will?...If I don't work all these hours people will think I'm lazy and they already don't like me, so I don't want to give them anything else to say about me... I never do anything right...What's wrong with me?" You know...those kind of thoughts. Those are intrusive. No one wants to sit around thinking like that all day, but it's what can happen when you're struggling.

The grieving process sounds awful because it is. But, once you get to acceptance it gets better. We talked about acceptance earlier in the book, because it's ultimately where you need to get to when it comes to your mother. This is the point where you know and understand who you are dealing with and that she is not going to change unless she makes the commitment to do so on her own. It's also the place where you make peace with it.

Activity:

Acceptance is the goal of the grieving process, but there's a journey to getting there. So, guess what time it is? Grab your journals and let's get to it! I only have one journaling prompt for you this time, but it's a doozy. Here it is...Be angry! Tell your mom everything you think and feel about her. Don't hold any punches. Set her ears on fire! Rip those pages to shreds if you need to, but get it all out. Then, after you've ranted, raged and cried, tell her that you forgive her. It doesn't matter whether you feel like saying that or not. You don't even have to feel ready to forgive her. Remember, she can't see your journal. This is for you. This is going to open up a flood gate of emotions. If it gets too hard, stop. Remember that whatever you're feeling is ok. But, you don't want to get stuck in your emotions. You don't want to remain in those feelings. If you get stuck, don't try to get out alone. Find someone you can talk to.

_____

_____

_____

_____

_____

_____

_____

_____

_____

_____

_____

_____

Section 6 Session 3
The First Step to Freedom

Most people think that forgiveness is the final goal. Unfortunately, that's not the case. Forgiveness is just the first step to freedom. After you've forgiven, you still have to heal from the damage that was done. You must forgive your mother for not being the person you needed her to be, but it doesn't stop there. Several of my clients have had to take care of their mothers at the end of their lives. They made amends in the end. Their moms apologized for treating them the way she did and everything!

So, my clients thought that was the end of it. They figured that the apology was what they were waiting for and now they could move on with lives and finally be happy. The problem comes in where you have forgiven, but you don't understand why you're still struggling and hurting. You don't realize it's because of the damage that was done before the forgiveness. Forgiveness releases you from the painful emotions and the stronghold your mother had on you. However, it does not cancel out the fact that there were only a few moments out of your entire life that she was kind to you. For those of you whose mother's a still living, I'm hoping to save you from this, by doing the work beforehand.

Healing from the damage may take you back through the grieving process, whether your mother is living or not. But this work is not really about grieving. It's about finding who you are outside of a title. You may be a mom, wife, professor, minister even...but who are you? Who did you want to be before you were told you weren't smart enough, before you had children, before life hit you? What dreams have you given up on? You may have to go back to the time in your life before your first heartbreak to remember who you were, so you can find out who you are.

If you eliminated all the opinions of other people, what would you say about yourself? Hopefully, you now have some insight about this from your previous journaling activity. What is it that makes you light up? What gives you a sense of worth? Even if you think you've missed your timing, I want you to go back there and allow yourself to live in a moment where you had hope. You will need something to hold on to while you're processing and healing the damaged places. What I mean is that you will need something to look forward to in order to keep yourself moving forward. It can be really easy to get stuck in the past when you start doing this kind of work. This is also why I suggest counseling if you haven't been. You may need someone to walk with you through this process.

Your damaged places may be different from others, but self-esteem is one thing that all of you will need to work through if you haven't done so already. As I've already mentioned in session 1 of this section, you likely have built-in self-esteem issues if your relationship with your mother has been tumultuous. Re-building self-esteem is not an easy task, because you have to be willing to take an honest look at yourself. You have to clear out all the voices trying to tell you who you are or are not, except your own voice. Self-esteem does not come from external sources. Meaning, no one can compliment you enough to give you self-esteem. When it comes from the outside, you become dependent on those sources to continue to lift you up. It has to come from inside of you. It's something that you have to know without a shadow of doubt, so that no one can take it away from you. You're going to have to build yourself up from the inside out. If you have faith, now is the time to draw from it.

Activity:

It's time to take a few minutes to complete the self-esteem building exercise on the next page.

Section 6 Session 3 Activity
Self-Esteem Building

List 3 things you like about yourself.

1. _____

   _____

2. _____

   _____

3. _____

   _____

Describe yourself in one word.

_____

Write one word you would want everyone in the world to call you.

_____

This is now your new mantra. Repeat everyday "I AM _____"

List 3 goals you would like to accomplish in the next five years.

1. _____

_____

2. _____

_____

3. _____

_____

If money and time were of no concern, what would you be doing right now?

_____

_____

_____

_____

_____

_____

_____

BELIEVER'S BUY-IN

Section 7 Session 1
"Your mother is a Believer too and she still don't like you?"

I'm neither a preacher nor a Bible scholar. I am simply a Believer just like you. I'm also a Christian who counsels. However, I don't bring faith into the counseling session unless my client brings it in first. This section is for Christians who struggle with having a relationship with your mom, particularly because of this scripture. Ephesians 6:2 says *"Honor your father and mother-which is the first commandment with a promise."*

We tend to believe that this scripture means that we are supposed to endure anything from our parents because we have to honor them as the Bible says. But I submit to you, that you should read this scripture in context. Often, we leave out verses 1 and 4. Read it in context. Ephesians 6:1-4 says *"Children, obey your parents in the Lord for this is right. Honor your father and mother-which is the first commandment with a promise-so that it may go well with you and that you may enjoy long life on the earth. Fathers, do not exasperate your children; instead, bring them up in the training and instruction of the Lord."*

I like the way the Amplified Bible lays out verse 4. It reads like this, *"Fathers, do not provoke your children to anger [do not exasperate them to the point of resentment with demands that are trivial or unreasonable or humiliating or abusive; nor by showing favoritism or indifference to any of them], but bring them up [tenderly, with lovingkindness] in the discipline and instruction of the Lord.*

Now, does this not give you a new perspective? It does to me. There were several commands within the scripture that flow together. If your mother is a Believer, then she has a part she is supposed to play as well. If she is not treating you like she should, then she is making it difficult for you to honor her. Of course, that does not give you a way out of your part. You still have to honor her in order to fulfill your commandment. Just remember that honoring her is so that you might have a good, long life; that part is not about her. You're not trying to keep her alive and well by honoring her. You're doing it because it keeps you alive and well.

Take Away:

You do not have to allow yourself to be abused or manipulated by your mother simply because either or both of you are Christian. You are not honoring anyone by allowing yourself to be hurt. Standing up for yourself is just as Christian as turning the other cheek. Forgiving someone does not mean that you forget. You forgive so that you can be released from the hold they have on you.

Section 7 Session 2
Honoring Her Shouldn't Bring Dishonor to You

I know what some of you are thinking; if she would just apologize everything would be ok. It could be water under the bridge and you could kiss and make up. The problem with this is that an apology from your mother may sound more like "sorry...not sorry". Especially if she feels like she's done nothing wrong or she is in denial. Have you heard apologies like this before? "Oh, you know I didn't mean it like that. You're the only one who took it that way. I didn't know you were so sensitive. I'm sorry you feel that way." An apology like that will leave you in a worse place than when you began.

What you're really looking for is an acknowledgement which sounds more like, "Yes, I did that and I said that. I wholeheartedly take responsibility for my words and my actions. I didn't know it affected you that deeply. My intention was not to hurt you. I can't take it back, but I will do my best to not let it happen again. Please forgive me."

I would take an acknowledgment over an apology any day, because at least I know the other person is truly sorry for what they have done. And more importantly, they realize the impact it had on me. But, you know your mother probably as good as or better than anyone. Chances are you will not get the acknowledgment or a heartfelt apology. However, you must still operate with honor and respect toward her.

Let me point out that we are to honor our parents for our own sake. The honoring is not actually for them. We, the children, are promised long life if we honor them. So, what does it mean to honor them? The Amplified Bible says to esteem; value as precious and be respectful toward them. But, what it does not say is that you have to dishonor yourself in order to honor them. When you think of honor think respect, but think about it on both sides. If your mother does not respect or honor you, it's going to be very difficult for you to honor and respect her. Don't put yourself in a position where you have to lie. If your mother is a meanie, then you don't have to tell people she's nice. That's lying not honoring! You can say she has a really strong personality that doesn't flow well with mine, so we have very short conversations. You can show her honor and respect as your mother by not telling everyone how nasty she is to you. But, that does not mean you have to be around her all the time.

You have the right to protect yourself. If you need to stay away and love and honor her from a distance, then do that. You will need to change your expectation of your mother. You know by now how she is going to respond to you. You pretty much know what she's going to say if she speaks to you at all. Or at least you know the tone she's going to use when she does speak to you. It's ok for you stay out of the line of fire. You do not need to tolerate being cursed at, talked down to or manipulated just for the sake of having a relationship with her. That's not a relationship anyway...it's abuse. Let's just call it what it is. It's mental and verbal abuse. No one has the right to abuse you, not even your mother. A relationship like that brings honor to no one.

Activity:

This next activity is going to take some time. I want you to write a short prayer that you can speak to God about often. Its purpose is to help you with how you feel about your mother as well as how to handle her behavior toward you. Remember that she has free will, so anything that you ask for on her behalf, she ultimately makes the decision over whether she wants to do it or not. On your mom's behalf, your focus should be praying God's will for her life. Your prayer is that she would be able to clearly hear him speaking to her, that her heart would be softened towards you and Him. Other than that, try to keep the prayer focused on yourself. This is your healing process. She will need to go through her own.

_____

_____

_____

Working Through Mommy Issues

Section 7 Session 3
You're Still on The Hook

You just read this in session 1 of this section, but I think it's worth repeating again. I love what the Amplified Bible says in verse 4, *"Fathers (parents), do not provoke your children to anger [do not exasperate them to the point of resentment with demands that are trivial or unreasonable or humiliating or abusive: nor by showing favoritism or indifference to any of them], but bring them up [tenderly, with loving kindness] in the discipline and instruction of the Lord."*

Ask yourself, does any of this sound like your mother? Does she provoke you to anger? Does she try to put demands on you that are trivial or unreasonable? Does she humiliate or abuse you? Does she show favoritism? Did she bring you up tenderly with love and kindness? Your mother has a part that she is supposed to fulfill in the scripture as well. If you're reading this book, I'm going to venture to say that your mother has not kept her part of deal. It doesn't mean that you are excused from doing your part. Remember, you are honoring your mother so that your life will be long. That's the promise made to you by God. But, it does not mean that you have to continue to subject yourself to pain.

It is ok to love and honor your mother from a distance, even if she's a Christian. Check on her. Make sure she has food, shelter and clothes. Those are things you can do to honor her. But, it does not mean you have to be the one go get the food, move her in with you or be the one to take her shopping for the clothes. As long as she has it you have honored her.

Be respectful and kind toward her. If you can only handle her in small doses, then do what you can do. Do not overextend yourself for her. In everything you do with or for her, make sure you have peace in doing it. If anything begins to disturb your peace then stop. In order to continue to honor her, you will have to be able to say "no" to her. Saying "no" is not being disrespectful. You have a right to do that. You are still a person with your own thoughts, feelings and emotions. And, they all matter. You do not need to deny yourself in order to honor your mother.

Here's something I want to leave with you before you finish the book. Who says that Christians can't go to counseling and continue to pray as well? I don't believe there's anything wrong with it. Counseling does not ask you to stop praying. It simply offers for someone to walk with you through your process until the answers to your prayers have manifested. Do not deprive yourself of the help you need for any reason. Also, do not subject yourself to unnecessary harm for any reason. Take care of yourself. If you don't, no one else will.

Attainable Skill:

Here is your final assignment. Think of 3 ways you can easily honor your mother without going out of your way. Incorporate her into your life instead allowing her to dictate yours. For example: If you are going grocery shopping for your own needs, ask if she needs you to pick up anything for her. You do not have to make an extra trip for her. You will have honored her simply by offering to pick something up for her. You honor her by continuing to show genuine love and respect for her.

Message From the Author

Thank you so much for reading this book! I hope it has been beneficial in helping you to better handle the relationship or lack of a relationship between you and your mother. Remember that this material was for you. Your mother needs a book or course of her own, but this one could be eye-opening for her. I hope that your healing process has begun in your life and I sincerely hope that the healing continues. Do not allow yourself to get so overwhelmed that you can barely see your way out before you reach out for help. As always, be proactive about your mental health, take care and God bless!

Need More Help?

Author Soneakqua J. White has created an online course as well as the workbook you just completed to assist you in your healing process. They are designed to help you deal with a mother who makes it difficult for you to care *for* and/or care *about* her. If you have ever asked yourself, "Why does my mother treat me the way she does?" this course is for you. If you find yourself wanting to scream out "Help, my mom doesn't like me!" this course is for you. If you spent the majority of your life trying to make your mother proud of you or just tried to survive being raised by her and you still have not succeeded…this course is for you. You will learn how to love yourself even though she didn't like you. You will learn to stop compromising your mental, physical, emotional and spiritual health to get someone to love you, who does not acknowledge your effort. Take your power out of her hands and live! Copy the link below in your URL to receive the coupon code for the online course.

https://www.udemy.com/working-through-mommy-issues/?couponCode=DOTHEWORK

Other Books by Soneakqua J. White

Get connected with
Author Soneakqua J. White on social media

 At the Table Counseling

 atthetablecounseling

 ATC_Counseling

… Working Through Mommy Issues

www.ingramcontent.com/pod-product-compliance
Lightning Source LLC
Chambersburg PA
CBHW071909070526
44583CB00016B/1916